Power Prayers FOR Little Hearts
After His Heart

Author
Penny Carlson

Illustrator
Leslie Ann Clark

ISBN : 978-1-961392-26-7 (Paperback)
        978-1-916770-87-4 (Hardcover)

Dedication

Thank you to my amazing husband, Alan, and our incredible sons and their beautiful wives, Joshua and Melissa, and Dustin and Jennifer. And our special blessing Derek Russell Thomas Tipton and his beautiful wife Julie. Thank you, God, for the greatest joys of my heart and life. Piper Rae, Madeleine Love, Bowie June, Dempsey Drew, and Christopher Drake Carlson. I am truly blessed. Our family rocks!

Power Prayers for Little Hearts

After HIS Heart

Penny Carlson   Leslie Ann Clark

Cookie Cutter Perfect

Jesus, You picked me before
I was even in my mom's tummy.
I know You have something special
for me to do.
Jeremiah 1:5

God, You made me inside my mom's tummy. Thank
You, God, for making me so amazing and wonderful. I
know everything you do, God, is so very awesome.
Psalms 139:13-14

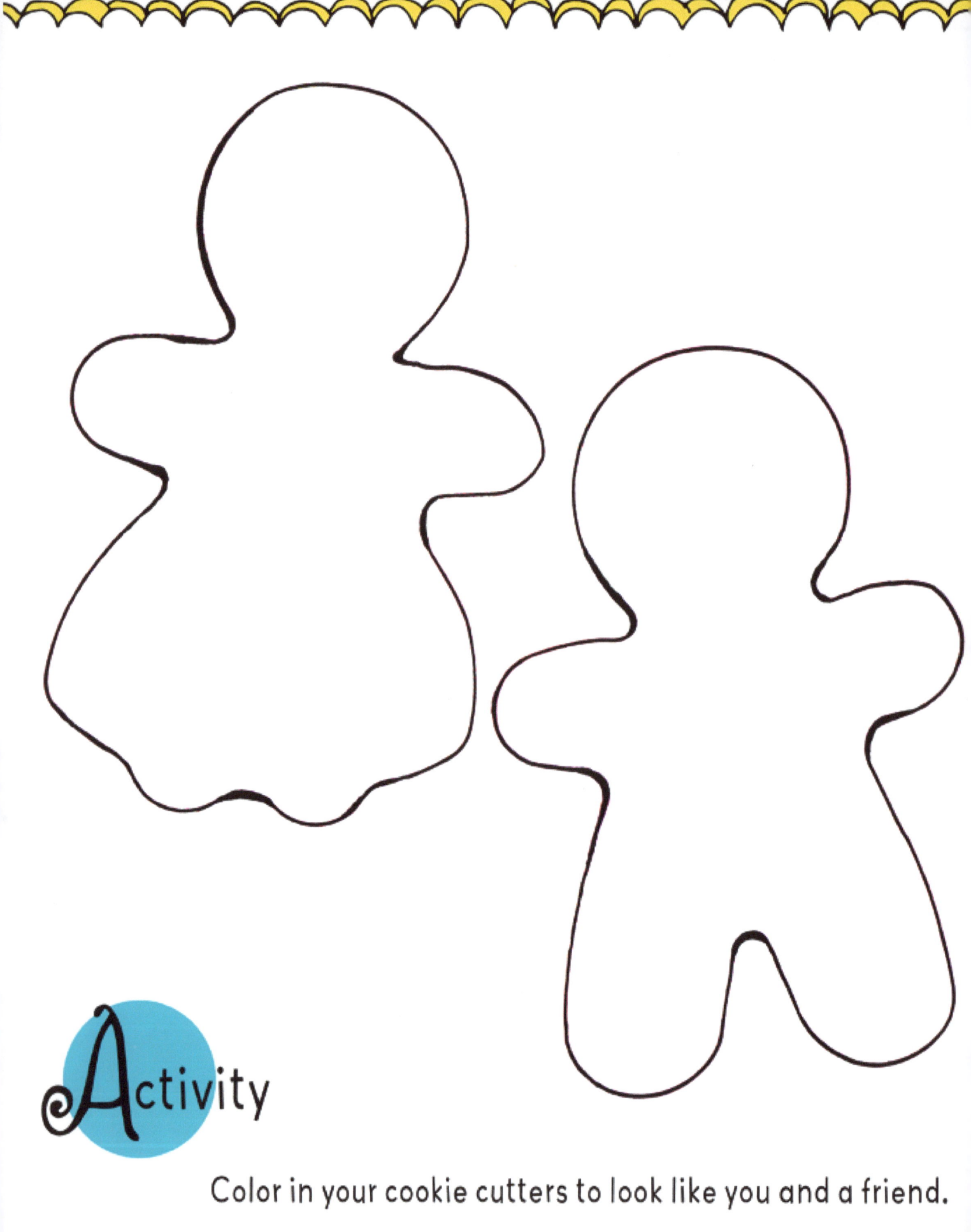

Color in your cookie cutters to look like you and a friend.

I know I am not too little to do what You asked me to do, because You said You would go with me.

Jeremiah 1:7

Thank You, God, for choosing me
even before this world was created.
You created me with Your love.
Thank You for choosing me to do
good things for You.
Ephesians 2:10

Obedience Brings Blessings

Thank You, God, for teaching me.
I'm a good listener. When I obey
Your Word I am full of joy.
Isaiah 54:13

I don't forget Your teachings.
I have a special place in my heart
for Your Word. Your Word keeps me
happy for a long time.   Proverbs 3:1-2

I listen to You and obey Your voice.
You will lead my feet in the way
You want me to go.   Proverbs 3:6

I obey my parents. I know, God, this is the right thing for me to do. I listen to them and show them honor and always love them. I have a very happy life because I choose to obey. Ephesians 6:1-2

I am a smart child and I make my dad and mom very happy! I make good choices. My parents have a good reason to be happy. Proverbs 23:24-25

Question

How do you please your parents?

Choices Choices

My heart chooses to do right.
I trust in You, God. You show me which
way to go and I obey Your Word.
Proverbs 3:5-6

I practice pleasing You
when I'm out at play or
all alone.
Deuteronomy 11:19

Question

Did you make a choice today?

I choose to do what is right, God,
and You make me very happy.
Psalms 17:15

I choose to do good things every chance I get.
I will learn what You want me to do, God, and
I choose to do those things.
Ephesians 5:15-16

I choose to listen
to good words. I
make good choices.
I pick friends who
love You too, God.
Psalms 1:1

Thinking Good Thoughts

I love how You think only the best thoughts about me, God. I choose to think only good thoughts about me too.

Psalms 139:17

You are my helper, God. Thank You for helping me think good thoughts that will please You.

I love You, God. I think about You when I wake up each day.

I think about You when I am splashing in my tub or pool.

I love to think about You when I sit down to eat.

I think about You when I go to sleep.

Psalms 139:24

I think about You God, whatever I do and wherever I go. You, God, will make my day great.

Psalms 1: 2 - 3

You know my thoughts before I think them.
Before I even say a word, God, You already
know what it is. I pray my thoughts and
my words will always be pleasing to You.

Psalms 139:2b

I'm careful what I think.
I choose to think thoughts that
are true. I won't listen to lies.
My thoughts will lead me.

Proverbs 4:23-24

 **Q**uestion

What good thoughts are you
thinking today?

Happy To Help

I do everything with a happy heart. I know You want me to be happy in everything I do. Thank You, Jesus, for giving me a happy heart. Colossians 3:23

I do all my chores with a happy heart. When I help people that You love, it makes You happy too! I am happy to do what I've been asked to do, just like I would be if I were doing it for You. Ephesians 6:7

I am a child of God. I do all my chores without fighting. I have a heart to help. I will choose to help joyfully. My heart is to please You, Jesus. Philippians 2:14-15

I'm Your child, God. You have called me to be a helper to all in need. I'm listening for Your voice. Speak to me and I will obey. 1 Samuel 3:10

I do for others, God, as You have done for me. I'm happy because I will be doing what You want me to do. John: 15-17

I Will Follow You

I taste and see that You, God, are good. I'm happy because I put my trust in You, God.
Psalms 34:8

I trust You, God.   You make my life full of joy.   Psalms 37:5

I follow Your Word. It guides my footsteps. You keep me safe when I sleep. I hear Your voice when I wake up. Thank You, God, for Your Word. It is like a flashlight that shows me which way to go and chases away the dark.
Proverbs 6: 22-23

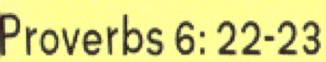

You are my Shepherd, God. You lead me down the right path. I choose to follow You and bring You honor.

Psalms 23:3b

Can you follow the path to Jesus?

Come

I do everything in love. My life is full of Your love.

1 Corinthians 16:14

estion   How do you follow Jesus?

Activity

Draw a picture of where you would like to go.

Be sure to take Jesus with you!

God Loves Children

Thank You, God, for loving me and
all the children of the world.
Psalms 107:31

Question   Do you know how much
God loves you?

 **Activity**

Draw a picture just for Him.

Power Pals With God

Jesus, You make me strong. I'm
full of Your awesome power.
Ephesians 6:10

I get my strength from You, God. When I
feel tired and weak I will trust in You, God.
I know You will make me strong again.
Isaiah 40: 29-31

I love You, God. I get my strength
from You. Your strength is a shield
around me.

Psalms 18:1-2

God, You are my rock, and You give me strength. I am like a deer that doesn't fall down. I stand strong when everything shakes around me. Psalms 18: 31-35

I do everything with Your power in me. Thank You, Jesus, for making me strong. Philippians 4:13

 **Question**   How does God makes you strong?

Blessing And Favor

I'm blessed when I'm in the city
and I'm blessed when I'm out in
the country.
WOW! That makes me blessed
wherever I am, and it's just because
I choose to obey You, God.
Deuteronomy 28: 2-3

Thank You, God, for Your favor.
You are a giant shield around me.
You keep me safe wherever I go.
Psalms 5:12

Thank You, God. I know
You and I love You. God,
You give me favor.
Proverbs 8:35

Color your very
own shield.

I'm blessed when I'm inside.
I'm blessed when I'm outside.

Dueteronomy 28:6

Thank You, God, for blessing me
with so many friends.

Activity

Color these faces to look like your family and friends.

Activity

Draw pictures of 5 ways God has blessed you.

FILL ME UP

God, Your love makes me patient. Your love in me makes it easier to say kind words. Your love fills me with self-control. Your love in me makes me want to tell the truth and not lie. Your love in me makes me happy when good things happen to others instead of me. Your love in me will never end. Your love in me gets stronger every day.
1 Corinthians 16:14

Thank You, God, for filling me up with Your love. Because You loved me first, I can love too. I will do my best to walk in Your love.
1 John 4:19-20

I will walk in love so that my words are not like banging my mom's pots and pans. If I give away all my toys and I have nothing left to play with, it won't make a difference unless I keep Your love in my heart.
1 Corinthians 13: 1-3a

 **Question** Do you love Jesus?

I choose to love my life, God.
I choose to love my brothers
and sisters and my friends
and neighbors.
Ephesians 5:2

I choose to do everything in love
because my life is full of Your love.
1 Corinthians 16:15

Draw a picture of Jesus.

I'm So Smart

You created me to be smart, God. I am getting smarter every day. You fill me with Your goodness.
Luke 2:40

I have Your wisdom, God. It comes straight from Heaven. Your wisdom teaches me what is important. I desire to please You, God. I am smart enough to know I can be patient and gentle just like You.
James 3:17a

Thank You, God, for pouring Your love on me. You fill me with wisdom and understanding so I am able to tell right from wrong.
Ephesians 1:8

I hear Your voice, God. I listen to Your Word.
I know what is good and right. I do what Your Word says I should do. I won't forget what I am taught.
Proverbs 4:1

I am stronger and smarter every day. I am more pleasing to You, God, and to other people too. Luke 2:52

uestion   How did God make you smart?

 **Activity**

Draw a picture of something that's right
and something that's wrong

Happy - That's Me

I choose to follow You, God. You make me so happy. I will follow You, God, and I will have a day full of fun.
Proverbs 8:32

I'm full of laughter. You make me so happy, Jesus. I will laugh today because You take good care of me.
Psalms 126:2

You made this day for me, God. I am so happy. I choose to be happy all day. I will laugh and have fun because You made this day for me.
Psalms 18:24

God, I wake up happy everyday, ready to laugh. You fill me, God, with happy thoughts.

Proverbs 8:30-31

Thank You, God, for filling my mouth with laughter. I will shout with joy.
Job 8:21

I'll Tell The World

I clap my hands and
shout to You, God, because
You are the very best.
Psalms 9:1

I sing songs
about You, God.
You make me so
happy. I will play and
sing today for You.
Psalms 33:3

I'll tell my friends how
awesome You are, God. I'll
sing about Your kindness and
praise You with everything in me.
Psalms 34:1-2

I will sing about the good things You do for me. I will tell about Your love for me in the morning and when I go to bed at night. I love You so much, God, and I will tell the world.

Psalms 92:1

I will sing to You, God. I will get down on my knees to tell You how much I love You. I am Your little lamb and You take good care of me.

Psalms 95:6-7

WOW! THANK YOU GOD!

Thank You, God, for friends and fun.
Thank You, God, for family too! My grandmas
and grandpas are pretty cool.

Draw something YOU are thankful for.

Thank God for it!

Thank You, God, for my legs to run and
jump. Thanks for birthdays to grow and
change. Thank You for the flag
and freedom.

Thank You for Christmas and Easter too.
I love to celebrate YOU!
Thank You for vacations, splashing pools,
and pumpkins too.
Thank You, God, for play time and a wonderful
mind to pretend.
Thank You for bicycles, boats, trains and planes.
Thank You, God, for the food we eat.
Cake and cookies can't be beat.

Activity

Draw a line from each picture to its matching picture.

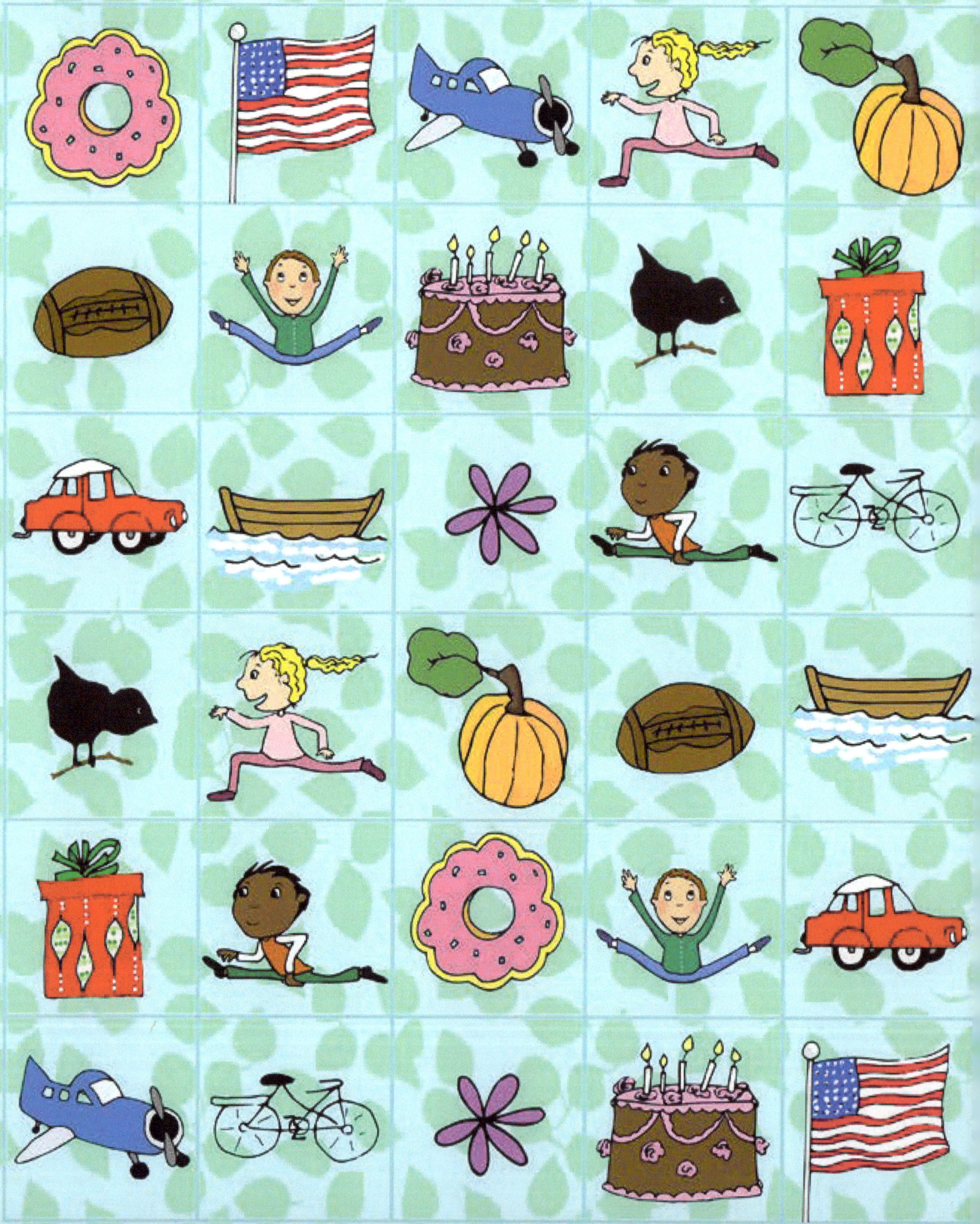

Thank YOU, GOD!

God, thanks for being with me when I'm in school.
Thanks for games, and all the fun times You give me.
Thank You for the rain and snow. I know it
helps to make Your beauty grow.
Thank You, God, for all the animals, big and small,
for butterflies and birds, ponies, puppies, kitties,
and silly goats too.

You truly are the very best, God,
From beginning to end, You thought
of everything. Wow!! Thank You, God!
You didn't forget anything at all!

Thank You , God, that You love me so-so-so much. Thank You that You sent Your Son, Jesus, to die on a cross for me and everybody. I choose to believe in You, God, and in Your Son, Jesus. Someday I will get to live forever in a place called Heaven.

John 3:16

From the author
Penny Carlson

Dear God, My prayer is that Your precious little ones would know You in such a real way, that they would have confidence and always be sure of who they are, and Whose they are in Christ Jesus. Show them how valuable they are in You.